WE NEED TO (TALK) ABOUT DEATH

NEON  SQUID

CONTENTS

INTRODUCTION

Hi, I'm Sarah. Allow me to be your personal guide, or "psychopomp," to the fascinating world of death! Together, we'll explore the science and history around death, funerals, and the afterlife. But more importantly, we'll learn how to have a **healthier relationship** with death and grief, so we can feel more confident about supporting ourselves and the people we care about.

Often when people think about death and dead bodies they feel afraid or sad (and that's OK because those feelings are normal!), but in the pages of this book I want to show you that these things can also be seen as **magical and powerful**. They can even help change the world for the better.

Death is something everyone experiences at some point, but not many people are comfortable talking about it. Mostly this is because they don't know how to, or because they're afraid of saying the wrong thing. This can leave a lot of people feeling scared and uncomfortable because they don't know what to expect when someone dies. It's important to talk about death because it is **a big part of life**. This book is a place you can turn to for answers and information about death and grief, about what is normal, what to expect, and ideas for things you can do to help yourself and others when they are grieving.

I want you to know that being curious about death and how it shapes our lives is **completely normal**. In fact, the work of countless artists, musicians, poets, inventors, and great thinkers has been inspired by their own questions about death.

So let's talk about death!

Your psychopomp,

Sarah Chavez

WHAT IS
DEATH?

Everything in nature that is alive, including plants, animals, and humans, will eventually die and make room for new life. For people, death is what happens when our bodies stop working. The heart stops beating, the lungs stop breathing in oxygen, the brain no longer works, and we can no longer communicate.

It may help you to understand the science of death by first understanding what humans are made of. And it might surprise you: we are made of stardust! In fact, everything that exists here on Earth was created from residue left from exploded stars. "The nitrogen in our DNA, the calcium in our teeth, the iron in our blood, the carbon in our apple pies were made in the interiors of collapsing stars," explains astronomer Carl Sagan.

This means that we may die, but the things that we are made of live on. All of the energy that was inside us is just transformed into other forms of energy, which become part of other things.

THE ELEMENTS INSIDE YOU WERE CREATED IN STARS BILLIONS OF YEARS AGO.

Not long ago, death was a familiar part of our lives. Almost everyone died at home and their bodies were looked after by their families and community. While this still happens, it's only in very recent history that death has largely been moved out of our homes and into places like hospitals and funeral homes. As a result, many of us no longer know what death and dead bodies look like, and when we don't know what to expect we often imagine things that are scary.

Learning the facts, science, and history about something you're afraid of, like death, can not only help you understand it, but also make it less scary. In fact, thinking and talking about death can actually make you happier! Modern-day studies have proved that ancient philosophers were correct all along: being

aware that we have a limited amount of time to enjoy our lives motivates us to live better. We can spend our time doing things that feel truly meaningful with the people we genuinely care about.

Everyone dies, so being curious about death is natural. However, because so many people are unfamiliar with death and don't have the skills to talk about it, they can feel uncomfortable or awkward. But that's OK, we all feel that way sometimes! This is why it's a good idea to find someone Aisha Adkins calls a "death buddy"—a designated person who is comfortable talking about death with you. You can ask each other questions, share your concerns and fears, or talk about the things that interest you with your death buddy.

SADNESS

LONGING

HOPELESSNESS

REGRET

ANGER

IT'S NORMAL TO FEEL DIFFERENT EMOTIONS

CONFUSION

FRUSTRATION

RELIEF

JOY

WHAT IS
GRIEF?

Grief is the feeling we have after someone dies. Many different emotions are part of grieving. Some people think that there are different stages of grief everyone goes through, but because everyone grieves differently, there's no right way to do it! Being happy or laughing while grieving doesn't mean you aren't grieving "properly" or that you don't love or miss your person. The truth is that grief is hard, and sometimes it can feel unbearable. Most of all, grief is an expression of our love.

SAYING THE WRONG THINGS

Because people don't talk about death very much, it can be hard to know what to say or do to support someone who is grieving. As a result, people who are trying to be kind sometimes say things that hurt instead of help. Here are a few things you should avoid saying to someone who is grieving.

"YOU NEED TO GET BACK TO NORMAL"

What's "normal" in your life will always be changing—where you live, who your friends are, and your likes and dislikes. So when someone dies, things change. There's no "normal" to return to.

"DON'T CRY, YOU NEED TO BE STRONG"

Not true: crying is good for you! It's our body's way of helping us release emotions that we may be struggling to get out. That's why we often feel better after crying.

"YOU SHOULD BE OVER IT BY NOW"

Some amount of grief will always stay with us, just as the love we have for someone always stays with us, too.

HOW TO HELP

When someone you care about is sad, the first thing you probably think about doing is cheering them up. It may seem strange, but the thing that will help a grieving person the most is letting them be sad. When we do this, we're acknowledging that their pain is real. As grief expert Megan Devine says, "some things cannot be fixed; they can only be carried." We can't fix grief, but we can help the people we care about carry their grief by listening to them. Sometimes the best thing we can say is something that acknowledges the truth, such as: "I know you're hurting, but I am here for you."

In the past, some African Americans decorated stoneware jugs with small objects. These either belonged to the person who died or were things that they would enjoy.

RIP tees originated within Black communities in the USA. They celebrate a person's life and make their loss visible in a society that often overlooks their deaths.

During the Victorian era people would make jewelry using the hair of the deceased.

MAKING A
MEMORIAL

Throughout history people have created memorials to remember their dead. These objects can be personal keepsakes, art, statues, or even buildings that honor a person or a historical event in which many people died. Here are some of the things people have created to remember those they love.

In Thailand families create memorial books containing information about the deceased person's life, photographs, stories, and even their favorite recipes.

Roadside memorials, or descansos, originated in Mexico as places where funeral processions could rest. Today they mark the places where people have died.

WHAT YOU CAN DO

There are plenty of things you can create to keep the memory of someone you love alive. The special memorial or items you make can also help you to continue sharing your thoughts and feelings about the person you're grieving. Here are a few ideas.

Decorate a box that can hold special items that remind you of your person. Later, take your box out to look at the objects, and share stories about them and how you are feeling.

Altars are spaces that can be created anywhere using things that are meaningful to you, such as photos, letters, small gifts, or candles.

Create a memorial flower or vegetable garden, or start off with a single potted plant you keep indoors that reminds you of your person.

REMEMBERING PETS

Pets are an important part of our families. We share our lives with them, make memories together, and comfort each other, so it makes sense that we feel a deep sense of grief when they die. Because of this, people have always honored their beloved animals in many of the same ways they have done for people. This includes burying them with grave goods, holding funerals, and making memorials for them.

"If you truly love a dog it will always live on" —Edna Clyne-Rekhy, author of *The Rainbow Bridge*

ANCIENT DOGS

Ancient Romans wrote short messages called epitaphs to remember their pets. In them, they shared important details about the animals and expressed their grief. One example reads: "I am in tears while carrying you to your last resting place, as much as I rejoiced when bringing you home in my own hands fifteen years ago."

PET FUNERALS

Around the world there are funeral homes and cemeteries just for pets. For example, in Bangkok, Thailand, people can bring their animals to a temple where Buddhist monks carry out full funeral rites to ensure a pet's good afterlife.

FINAL STOP

When Japan's popular feline stationmaster, Tama, died in 2015, thousands of people attended her funeral. The train company credited their success to Tama, so they created a shrine to her memory at the station, which is even shaped like a cat in her honor!

WHAT HAPPENS TO A DEAD BODY?

It's normal to miss your loved ones and want to know what's happening to them, and that feeling doesn't stop when someone dies. So it makes sense that one of the most common questions is: What is happening to their body? Just as the Earth has nurtured us throughout our lives—nourishing our bodies with food, water, and sunshine—when we die our bodies return to the Earth through a process called decomposition.

IT'S IMPORTANT TO KNOW THAT, WITH RARE EXCEPTIONS, DEAD BODIES ARE PERFECTLY SAFE TO TOUCH AND BE AROUND.

THE PROCESS BEGINS

Just minutes after we die, the decomposition process begins inside our bodies. Although a person is dead, their physical body, also called a corpse, will soon become a diverse ecosystem, full of life! Looking at the outside of a person's body, the only physical changes you will notice at this time are that their muscles appear to be relaxed.

BREAKING DOWN

Now that the body no longer creates heat and energy, the skin will become cool to the touch. With the heart no longer working, blood slowly begins to settle in the parts that are closest to the ground. Chemical reactions begin breaking down everything inside.

STIFFENING

Three to six hours after death, those very relaxed muscles will begin to stiffen due to chemical changes happening within the body. This stage of decomposition is called rigor mortis, from Latin words meaning "stiffness of death." This stage only lasts about a day or two before the muscles relax completely again.

BACTERIA GET TO WORK

Bacteria break down the body further, filling it with fluid, and releasing gas and waste. This causes the abdomen to bloat and the skin to change colors. Small noises, which sound a bit like a stomach rumbling, might come from the body. At this stage decomposition may be sped up by a variety of helpers, such as flies and beetles.

THE SKELETON EMERGES

Once fluids, gas, and waste have left the body, what remains (skin, muscles, and tissues) begins to dry out, and the skeleton starts becoming exposed. This process can take a number of years. The speed of decomposition varies greatly and is largely influenced by the type of environment the body is in.

AT THE **FUNERAL HOME**

EMBALMING

Sometimes, families will have their person embalmed. In this process an embalmer will drain all of the fluids and blood from inside the body and replace them with a chemical solution. This slows down the decomposition process. Embalming can be helpful if a body needs to be sent to a different country, or a family needs extra time to travel for a funeral.

A funeral home provides services and support for the dead and their families. The people who work in funeral homes, called funeral directors, provide assistance like preparing the body or making arrangements for the funeral. When a person dies, a funeral home may pick up the person's body in a special vehicle and transport it to the funeral home, where it is placed in a large refrigerator to slow down decomposition. When it's time, the funeral director will then bring out the body to prepare it for a viewing, burial, or cremation. This can involve washing the person's body and hair, shaving them, dressing them in clothes, or putting makeup on them, before placing their body in a casket (see pages 32–33).

THE HISTORY OF EMBALMING

Modern embalming was invented during the American Civil War (1861–1865) to slow down decomposition long enough to send the soldiers' bodies home to their families for burial. Embalmers would sometimes display embalmed bodies in upright coffins near the battlefield as a way to advertise their services.

WHAT IS A
FUNERAL?

A funeral is an event where people gather to honor someone who has died. Funerals give us an opportunity to support their family, express our grief, and perform cultural or religious rituals to ensure that the deceased person has a good afterlife. They can also restore dignity to an individual who may have been denied it in life, and strengthen our connections to others.

Funerals are as unique as people are—they can be quiet and formal, or loud and joyful like a party. Death is an important part of life's story, so, when possible, a funeral will reflect who a person was and the things that were important to them.

VIEWING

A viewing is a time before a person's body is buried or cremated, when people can spend time with their person's body, perform meaningful rituals, and say goodbye.

A CELEBRATION OF LIFE

A funeral can be known by different names, such as service, memorial, celebration of life, or homegoing. It can take place in a religious space, like a church or temple, at a funeral home, or at someone's house. People may pray, play music, dance, or share stories about the person who died. If the person is to be buried, the funeral might include a procession to the cemetery. Like the funerals themselves, processions can look very different! Some consist of a quiet line of cars, while others look similar to a parade, with people carrying the casket through the neighborhood.

REPAST

A repast is a meal immediately following a funeral where people spend time together and share memories. This more casual, social activity provides mourners with the time and space to transition back into their daily lives, supported by their community.

In New Orleans, USA, funeral processions are celebrations that uphold ancestral traditions and honor the lives of those who have died.

HEAVEN

Several religions believe there is a place located beyond our sight or perception in the sky called Heaven. It is imagined as a world similar to the one we live in on Earth, but free of problems. Here, people feel peaceful and are reunited with those they love.

WHERE WILL
I GO?

While we know what happens to our bodies when we die, humans have always wondered if the thing that makes us uniquely us, like a spirit or personality, continues to exist in an afterlife. This question has resulted in different societies across the world believing in different afterlife destinations. In the end, the one afterlife we know about for certain is the one we create here on Earth, through our love and how we choose to remember someone.

THE LAND OF TWO FIELDS

Ancient Egyptian people had elaborate afterlife beliefs. When a person died it was thought they would go through many rituals to reach the afterlife. These included the weighing of the heart, performed by the god Anubis, who had the body of a human and the head of a jackal. If found worthy, spirits could enter an afterlife called the Land of Two Fields.

MICTLAN

Before Europeans colonized North America, some indigenous communities in what is now Mexico believed that the way a person died would determine how they spent their afterlife. For example, those who died in battle would transform into hummingbirds or butterflies. Most would travel to a dark but peaceful land known as Mictlan. Spirits would encounter many obstacles on the way there, including crossing a difficult mountain range and coming face-to-face with jaguars, before coming to rest in the land of the dead.

AQUAMATION AND
CREMATION

Instead of being buried in the ground, some people choose to be cremated. There are two methods for cremating a dead body: one using fire, called cremation, and the other using water, known as aquamation. Both of these processes break down the muscles, tissues, and bones of the body. When each process is complete, what's left looks similar to the ashes you see in a fireplace once a fire has burned out, along with some small bone fragments.

CREMATION

Bodies are first prepared for cremation by removing any large medical devices, such as pacemakers or prosthetic limbs. Next, each person's body is given a metal identification tag and placed in a cardboard or wooden casket. Then it is placed inside a giant, noisy machine called a retort. The extremely high temperatures inside the retort work to vaporize the soft tissues and reduce the body to bones and ashes in about two hours.

CREMATION CEREMONY

Did you know that you can ask to be present at a cremation? This is called a "witness cremation." Many Japanese families perform a special ritual during a cremation called a *kotsuage*. Family members use long chopsticks to pick up bone fragments and place them into an urn.

AQUAMATION

In this process, sometimes referred to as water cremation, the body is laid in a metal cradle before being inserted into the aquamation chamber. Alkaline water and heat work to gently break down the body. After eight hours only brittle bones and ashes remain. Aquamation is considered a more environmentally friendly option than cremation because there are no carbon emissions and it uses 90% less energy.

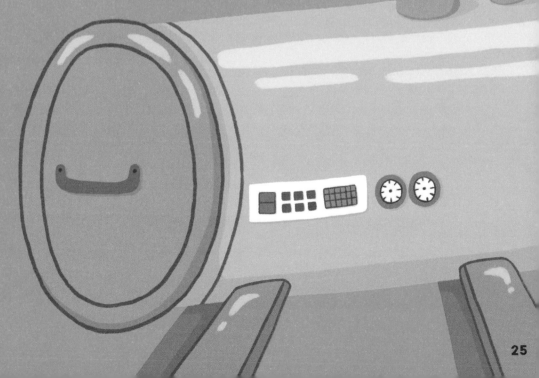

ALL ABOUT
ASHES

After someone is cremated, what is left behind is about 5 lb (2 kg) of ashes and small pieces of bone. Flame-cremated ashes are usually light gray in color, while aquamated ashes are much whiter. The ashes are gathered and placed inside a clear plastic bag with a round metal tag that identifies the person. The bag is then placed in a black plastic container before being returned to the family.

A metal tag identifies the deceased.

SCATTERING ASHES

A common thing to do with ashes is to scatter them in a special location. Sometimes people will leave instructions for what they want done with their ashes, like scattering them in their favorite place. There are rules about where you can place ashes safely, so it's important to get permission first.

URNS

Most people keep ashes inside an urn (a vase made especially to hold them). However, ashes can be stored in any container you find meaningful or that reminds you of your person, like a favorite cookie jar. It's a good idea to make sure your chosen container has a lid, in case your cat accidentally knocks it over!

MARVELOUS AFTERLIFE

Before Marvel comic book writer Mark Gruenwald died he asked for his ashes to be mixed into ink. It was then used to print a special issue of a comic he had worked on!

Can a tree or plant grow from ashes? No. While it's a lovely idea to plant someone's ashes with a tree or flowers, it's more of a symbolic gesture. Cremated remains aren't compatible with healthy soil and can actually harm plants.

SPECIAL GOODBYES

Artists and companies can transform ashes into special keepsakes, too:

Baby you're a firework!

A pyrotechnics company can create a special firework using about three tablespoons of cremated remains.

Play it again

Music lovers can have someone's ashes pressed into a vinyl record that can play music or a voice recording.

Shine like a diamond

In special laboratories cremated remains can even be turned into diamonds!

IN THE
CEMETERY

Cemeteries are wonderful places to enjoy nature and spot different types of wildlife.

A cemetery is a place where the remains of dead people are buried or interred, which is when a dead body is placed in a grave or tomb. People visit cemeteries for lots of different reasons, not just to attend a funeral. A cemetery is a bit like an outdoor museum, an art gallery, a community center, and a nature reserve all in one!

You might see people cleaning graves and leaving offerings such as flowers, gifts, food, or drinks.

TYPES OF CEMETERY

Some cemeteries look like gardens with beautiful statues, while others with flat grave-markers resemble parks. There are cemeteries that support different religious and cultural practices, which require specific burial methods or rituals, while other cemeteries were created as a result of racial segregation.

At some cemeteries you can take a guided tour, attend a music or theater performance, or watch a movie!

THINGS TO SPOT

When you visit a cemetery you may encounter different symbols or pictures marked on the tombstones. Each picture tells a story, and many of them have hidden meanings.

The Star of David is a symbol of the Jewish faith.

Anchors symbolize hope and safety.

This death's-head reminds the living of their mortality.

With its drooping branches, a willow tree indicates mourning.

Two hands clasped together means love and connection.

GOING
GREEN

Green burial is a new name for something very old—burying a body directly into the earth in a shroud or casket made of materials that won't harm the environment. This is how people have been buried throughout human history. It allows the body to return to the earth so that it can become part of nature. Other forms of burial are not as eco-friendly.

A hole is dug, sometimes by the family and friends of the deceased person.

GREEN BURIAL

Why do people choose green burial? People of Muslim and Jewish faiths have always practiced this type of burial for religious reasons. Others want a green burial because they love nature, and protecting the environment is important to them.

The body is placed in natural materials that are safe for the environment.

The body is placed onto wooden boards and strong ropes that lay across the top of the grave.

People then take hold of the ropes to gently lower the body into its final resting place.

No tombstone is used so that nature can thrive, but the grave can be marked with a plant or stone.

MODERN BURIAL

Starting in the 1920s, many cemeteries began using burial methods to make taking care of the grass easier and to prevent the ground over coffins from shifting. This form of burial is sometimes chosen for religious reasons, or because someone wants to be buried with members of their family who are already in a particular cemetery.

UNFORTUNATELY MODERN BURIALS CAUSE HARM TO THE ENVIRONMENT.

The grave is lined with steel, concrete, or plastic.

Modern caskets are usually made of materials that are built to last and will not break down naturally.

Gravediggers use a large metal device to lower the casket into the grave.

Once a grave is filled, the grass is arranged on top. Later, a grave marker or tombstone will be installed.

COFFINS, CASKETS, AND SHROUDS

Before they're buried, people are placed in a coffin or a casket, or they're wrapped in a fabric shroud. Coffins are smaller at the feet and wider at the shoulders, whereas caskets are a rectangle shape and look like a box.

SHROUDS

A shroud, or "winding sheet" as it has been called in the past, is a large piece of fabric that is wrapped around a body before it is buried or cremated. Shrouds are more common around the world than caskets or coffins, and they can be customized with embroidery, felting, or other types of handiwork.

A GHOST IS OFTEN DEPICTED IN A **WHITE SHEET** BECAUSE OF SHROUDS!

COFFINS

Many coffins are made out of natural materials, making them ideal for green burial. Some families choose a cardboard coffin and invite friends and family to help decorate it with art and photos. A type of stone coffin often found inside tombs is called a sarcophagus, which means "flesh-eater."

CASKETS

Caskets are typically made of wood, metal, and synthetic materials. There are many different types and styles of caskets, from ones with built-in windows so you can see the person's face, to fancy gold-plated caskets, and even caskets that feature your favorite sports team!

FANTASY COFFINS

In Ghana, Africa, people can have a special, hand-carved wooden casket made for them that reflects their personality. These caskets are called fantasy coffins. They can come in any shape you can imagine—be it an animal, a car, or a vegetable! What would your fantasy coffin look like?

GRAVE GOODS

Grave goods are items that are buried or cremated with a body. These objects can range from supplies, including food, tools, and magical items, to gifts and even animal companions! Sometimes people choose their own items to take with them before they die, like photographs. Other times friends and family members will place gifts or letters in the coffin. Grave goods can help mourners feel more connected to the person who died, and reassure them that the deceased person will have everything they need in the afterlife.

GRAVE ROBBERS

Discovering grave goods can tell us a lot about an ancient culture, but is it ever OK to dig up a grave without permission? After all, we'd probably be uncomfortable with someone digging up the grave of our grandmother and placing her in a museum, yet this sort of thing happens. Those most vulnerable to grave robbing are typically people who have fewer rights because of prejudices about their race, religion, or culture.

TONGUE AMULETS

In China during the Han Dynasty, people would place a piece of jade carved into the shape of a cicada on the tongue of a person before they were buried. It was believed that the jade would help slow down decomposition, while the cicada was a symbol of rebirth.

MASK OF THE RED QUEEN

This mask—made of jadeite, shells, and obsidian—was placed over the face of a Maya noblewoman when she was buried. She was given the nickname "The Red Queen" when her tomb was uncovered in Mexico and found to be covered in a bright red substance called cinnabar.

TERRACOTTA WARRIORS

Before he died, Qin Shi Huang, the first emperor of China, had many grave goods built to protect him in the afterlife. They included replicas of horses and chariots, and more than 8,000 life-size warrior figures! These are known as the terracotta warriors.

MIRRORS

The Etruscans, an ancient culture from Italy, buried their dead with many items, including mirrors. The mirrors were often decorated with pictures that showed scenes from daily life or inscriptions of words.

Pieces for a board game were found in a burial mound in Norway. Archaeologists believe the game pieces were used to play an ancient Roman board game similar to chess.

STEP INSIDE A
MAUSOLEUM

A mausoleum, also known as a tomb, is an above-ground building where corpses are interred. Mausoleums can hold one body or several. The bodies are usually placed into small casket-size spaces, which are then sealed shut. World leaders, historic figures, and royalty have often been placed in mausoleums. In some places, including Russia, Vietnam, and China, people can visit and see the embalmed bodies of former leaders on display.

The Taj Mahal in India was built to house the body of the wife of the emperor.

Egyptian pyramids contain tombs and grave goods for the afterlife.

If you visit your local cemetery you may see mausoleums that look like this.

COLUMBARIUMS

Columbariums are buildings or rooms for storing cremated remains. Many columbariums look like museums or churches inside, complete with marble floors, art, and colorful stained glass windows.

Some columbariums allow families to display personal items alongside the urn.

SPENDING TIME WITH LOVED ONES

In Manila, a city in the Philippines, some wealthy families choose to build mausoleums that look similar to houses. These structures can even contain air conditioning, kitchens, and furniture so that the living can comfortably spend time with their dead: cooking, sharing meals, or watching TV.

The outside of this Japanese columbarium looks like a traditional Buddhist temple, but all is not as it seems... Inside it looks like you've been transported to a futuristic world, with LED lights on the walls and glowing crystal Buddha statues!

OSSUARIES AND CATACOMBS

An ossuary is a place where human bones are kept. They can be as small as a box or as large as a building, which is why they're sometimes called "bone houses." The bones are often displayed like art, stacked or arranged in unique ways. A catacomb is like an ossuary, but underground.

THE SEDLEC OSSUARY

In Czechia there is a church elaborately decorated with bones, known as the Sedlec Ossuary. It houses the remains of more than 40,000 people, which were used to create several bone pyramids and a large chandelier made from skulls and bones!

THE PARIS CATACOMBS

Beneath the city streets of Paris, France, the dead rest in a network of catacomb tunnels. The catacombs are decorated with the bones of millions of people who once walked the city streets above. The entrance sign reads: *Arrête! C'est ici l'empire de la Mort* (Halt! This is the empire of Death).

THE CATACOMBS RUN UNDERNEATH PARIS FOR ABOUT 200 MILES (320 KM).

LAND, SEA, AND SKY

There's more than one way to bury a dead body, and new choices become more widely available all the time. These different options are sometimes the result of scientific developments or cultural practices, but they can also be influenced by the different environments people live and die in, too. As a result, some of these burials incorporate elements like land, sea, or sky.

BURIAL AT SEA

In some places it's possible to be "buried" at sea by a boat. It is equipped with a slide that transfers the body into the water, where it can gently slip beneath the waves. Bodies are placed in metal caskets or weighted shrouds to ensure that they rest on the ocean floor.

SKY BURIAL

Some cultures leave bodies outside, allowing birds to take a part of the body with them as they fly off into the sky. While sky burials are practiced for a variety of reasons, many people view this ritual as a way to give themselves back to nature. It's a way of saying thanks for all the nourishment and joy nature has provided throughout their lives.

CORAL REEF BURIAL

Cremated remains can be mixed with concrete to create special reef balls. These are placed on the seafloor in areas where the ecosystem has been damaged. This practice creates habitats for sea creatures and encourages coral and algae to grow.

TREE BURIAL

When a baby dies in the remote village of Tana Toraja, Indonesia, it is carried to a tree at night by torchlight. A hole is carved into the living tree trunk, and the baby's shrouded body is placed inside.

COMPOSTING

The newest burial option, and one of the greenest, is composting. Bodies are laid inside vessels with wood chips and straw. Over the next few weeks, heat and microbes gently transform the body into rich soil that's returned to the family for them to scatter, use to plant a tree, or donate to a forest.

DESIGNING DEATH

FUTURE CEMETERIES

Imagine walking through a park at night. On the tree branches above you hang lanterns that light your way like stars. In this conceptual cemetery from the team at DeathLAB, the gentle glow of the lights doesn't come from electricity. Instead, bodies resting in special vessels are generating heat as they decompose. This heat is converted into the energy that lights the lanterns.

MUSHROOM BURIAL SUITS

Artist Jae Rhim Lee designed a burial suit made of mushrooms that could assist decomposition and help to transfer nutrients from the body to surrounding plant life. "The power of the suit is that it creates the need for meaningful planning and discussion around death," Lee said.

People are always inventing ways to make death care more meaningful, accessible, and environmentally friendly. Many of these things were designed to solve specific problems—like what to do in crowded cities where they're running out of space for burials, or how to create caskets without using resources that are bad for the environment. But perhaps the most important thing these new inventions do is help ignite our imaginations about what is possible and how, through death, we can create a better life for everyone.

SPECIAL TOMBSTONES

Artists have been commissioned to create unique tombstones that truly reflect the lives of the individuals buried beneath them. These include tombstones that cast rainbows, engraved QR codes that enable you to hear the person's voice, and even sculptures of beloved pets.

COULD TOMBSTONES OF THE FUTURE INCLUDE TOUCHSCREENS OR HOLOGRAMS?

SOOTHING SOUNDS

During a hospital stay, artist Yoko Sen observed that there were many unsettling sounds in a patient's environment, like machines beeping. Because of this, Sen created My Last Sound. This musical piece incorporates the sounds people say they most want to hear at the end of their lives, such as the ocean, laughter, and the voices of people they love.

ALL ABOARD!

The Necropolis Railway was a special train route operating in London from 1854 to 1941. It transported the dead and their families to the cemetery. After visiting the graveyard, people could have food and drinks in one of the many refreshment rooms at the cemetery's train station.

TRANSPORTING
THE DEAD

While some cultures prefer to keep their dead close to home by burying them nearby, many communities have burial grounds located farther away. As a result, people have created many different ways to transport their dead!

A STREETCAR NAMED DEATH

Before there were cars, people in cities could sometimes get around using a streetcar, or trolley. These small open-air buses were pulled by donkeys or horses in the 1800s, but were later powered by electricity. Many streetcars had funeral cars with special compartments to store coffins in.

Many funeral cars were painted in dark colors, had black velvet curtains, and even had stained glass windows to make them look like churches.

HEARSE

A hearse is a special kind of car designed to transport bodies. The back of the car is modified to be large enough to hold one or two coffins. These cars can be easily recognized by a unique s-shaped bar on the outside, called a landau bar.

FUNERAL CARRIAGE

While many horse-drawn funeral carriages were simple, some people thought that a person's final ride should be a special one! They designed fancy funeral carriages with large windows on each side, so that people could see the coffin or body inside as it passed through town.

PALLBEARERS

Pallbearers are the people who help carry a person's coffin at a funeral or a cemetery. While some funeral homes provide professional pallbearers, some families prefer to choose people who had a meaningful relationship with the deceased to carry them to their final resting place.

In some places, such as Ghana, Africa, carrying a coffin has become an art form that includes choreography and dancing.

45

DEATH FESTIVALS

OBON

Deceased Japanese ancestors are welcomed during Obon with a fire, offerings of food, and folk dances. When it's time to say goodbye, glowing lanterns are released at night to float along rivers and lakes to guide the dead home. They remind people that their loved ones will return again next year.

DAY OF THE DEAD

This festival, known as *Día de Muertos* in Spanish, has been celebrated by indigenous people in Mexico and parts of South America for centuries. During the festival it's believed that the spirits of the dead visit their living families, who welcome them by leaving offerings called *ofrendas* on altars, cleaning and decorating their graves, or flying large kites.

Around the world people remember their dead with food, music, and cultural rituals. These rituals can be as simple as lighting a candle and saying a prayer at home, or as elaborate as multi-day festivals requiring months of preparation. No matter how big or small the ritual, what matters most is that they help us to grieve, celebrate those we love, and reinforce the bonds between us that not even death can break.

ALL SOULS' DAY

Catholic people honor their dead on November 2—All Souls' Day. They attend a special service at church and visit cemeteries to clean graves and leave flowers. In Sicily, Italy, the spirits of the dead are believed to visit the homes of the living to leave children gifts of marzipan.

FAMADIHANA

The Malagasy people of Madagascar remove the bodies of their ancestors from their crypts each year. They reshroud them in silk and reinscribe their names so they will always be remembered. Then, in a ritual called "the turning of the bones," they dance with the dead in celebration and remembrance.

CREATE YOUR OWN MEMORY DAY

You can create your own special day to remember a loved one. It can be as simple as watching your person's favorite movie, or you could gather with others to share stories and memories.

FOOD AND DRINK

Ancient Romans put special devices into graves to deliver drinks, called libations, to the dead.

In parts of the UK and North America, funeral cookies were given out as an invitation to a funeral, or handed out as a keepsake afterward.

FOOD IDEAS

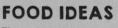

Throughout history people have used food to honor death, the dead, and their own grief. It's as though there is a special kind of magic when we join with others to remember our loved ones and mourn over a meal. Here are a few ideas for how you can remember loved ones with food.

Set an empty place with a plate of food at your table. This is something many different cultures do to mourn their loved ones.

People around the world mark life's most important moments with food and drink—whether it's cake for birthdays or a toast with champagne. When special food and drinks are included it lets people know that the occasion they're gathering for is a noteworthy one. For many cultures no meal or ritual is more important than a funeral feast. When food is shared it can help us feel more connected to each other, and to the person who has died.

Pan de Muerto is a sweet bread enjoyed by both the living and the dead during Day of the Dead.

During the Obon festival in Japan, people make vegetable animals for spirits visiting the world of the living to ride on back to the afterlife.

During the 19th century in Sweden, hard sugar candies shaped like little corpses and wrapped in paper were given out before funerals.

Eat in silence and, with adult supervision, burn a letter written to the dead, its words carried to the spirit world by smoke.

Cook your person's favorite dish or recipe using their cooking utensils, and share it with friends and family.

HERBS AND
FLOWERS

Did you know that flowers and plants have a language all of their own? In many cultures different flowers and herbs have their own special meanings and stories, and many of them are associated with death. People have used flowers and herbs to convey important messages: incorporating them into funerals, leaving them at graves as offerings, or using them to decorate the corpse before it is buried or cremated.

MARIGOLDS

Beautiful garlands of orange marigolds are often wrapped around bodies before they are cremated in India. In Mexico it's believed that their scent helps guide visiting spirits back to their earthly homes during Day of the Dead.

PERIWINKLES

These small, blue flowers were once used by African people who were enslaved in the USA to mark their graves, as they were not given materials to create grave markers. The periwinkles bloomed each year, showing the places where people had been buried.

CHRYSANTHEMUMS

In Japan, China, and Korea these flowers are associated with death and are almost exclusively used for funerals or during ancestor rites. Japanese funerals sometimes feature large flower displays that are arranged to look like ocean waves or mountains.

ROSEMARY

This fragrant herb symbolizes mourning and remembrance. Ancient Romans carried rosemary during funeral processions, before throwing it into the grave. Later, throughout Europe in the 20th century, people placed rosemary into the hands of the dead before burial.

PARSLEY

In ancient Greece parsley was planted over graves, and athletes would wear parsley crowns during Funeral Games. These were played in the deceased's honor, and are recognized as an inspiration for the Olympic Games.

MONJAS CORONADAS

In Spain and Mexico during the 18th century, nuns would sometimes be buried wearing large crowns of flowers, which symbolised immortality. When a nun died, a painter would create a portrait of her wearing the crown she was buried in. These paintings are called *monjas coronadas* (crowned nuns).

PAPA GEDE

Papa Gede is believed to be the first man who died in Haiti, a country in the Caribbean. He greets the souls of the newly dead at a crossroads, before escorting them to a place called Ginen to join their ancestors.

XOLOITZCUINTLE

Spirits traveling to Mictlan, the Mesoamerican land of the dead, are said to encounter an ancient, hairless dog known as a xoloitzcuintle. If the person had been kind to animals during their lifetime, the xoloitzcuintle guides them safely across a river.

THE
PSYCHOPOMPS

It's a comfort to think that when we die a helpful guide might be waiting to welcome and accompany us along our journey to the afterlife—this is the job of a psychopomp! These afterlife escorts come in a variety of forms, including animals and people, and are a feature of religions and cultures all over the world.

L'ANKOU

In Brittany, France, the reaper was known as L'Ankou and could be anyone—your uncle, your neighbor, or even you! It was believed that the last person buried in the local cemetery would inherit the job of guiding souls to the afterlife.

GRIM REAPER

You may already be familiar with the most famous psychopomp of all, whose image can be traced back to artwork depicting the Black Plague. The Grim Reaper appears as a skeleton wearing a hooded cape and carrying a scythe (once used by farmers to cut and harvest grains like wheat).

YAMA

Yama, the Hindu god of death, rides a buffalo and carries a rope, which he uses to pull souls out of their human bodies at the time of their deaths. Yama is believed to watch over the land of the dead.

MEET THE
MUMMIES

A mummified person, sometimes called a mummy, is a person whose body was preserved after death. Mummification delays the decomposition process. A person's corpse can be mummified intentionally by people using chemicals, or it can happen accidentally if the body was left in an environment that naturally mummified it.

HUMAN-MADE MUMMIES

Chances are, you're already familiar with ancient Egyptian people whose bodies were intentionally mummified, but have you ever wondered why people made mummies? Different cultures have preserved their dead for many reasons. For some it was to prepare them for a happy afterlife. For others, mummifying a body was a way for them to keep a loved person physically present and part of the community they once lived in.

In Papua New Guinea bodies are placed in a hut with a fire to produce heat and smoke, which dries them out.

The afterlife beliefs of the ancient Egyptians resulted in elaborate funerary rituals, including mummification.

ACCIDENTAL MUMMIES

Environmental conditions like temperature and moisture play a big role in how a body decomposes. When a person's corpse is exposed to just the right type of conditions a mummy can accidentally be created. For example, when water seeps into a coffin and reacts with the body's fat, a chemical process known as saponification occurs. This produces a waxy substance called adipocere on the body, creating what's known as a "soap mummy."

Bodies that were placed into bogs in Ireland turned into naturally made mummies.

ÖTZI WAS FOUND BY HIKERS IN 1991.

Ötzi the Ice Man's body was preserved more than 5,000 years ago by glacier ice and snow.

CORPSE MAGIC

Our bodies can do, feel, and create incredible things in life, but some people believe they can also accomplish wondrous things in death! In just about every part of the world you can find stories about corpses that possess extraordinary magical powers and abilities: corpses that can heal the sick or protect warriors in battle, and spirits who give advice to politicians from beyond the grave.

ÑATITAS

In La Paz, Bolivia, some Aymara people keep skulls called *ñatitas*, which translates to "little pug-nosed ones," in their homes. It's believed that they can heal, grant wealth or success, and solve crimes. The skulls act as vessels for the spirits of those who once lived, and are cherished like members of the family. *Ñatitas* are often given hats to keep them warm and sunglasses to protect their sight.

CORPSE MEDICINE

Early European doctors used corpses to try to cure illnesses, pain, and diseases. Patients were prescribed concoctions that contained blood, powder from ground-up human skulls, or the powdered remains of ancient Egyptian people who were mummified.

BEJEWELED SKELETONS

Have you ever seen a skeleton covered in jewels? You might if you visit a Catholic church in Germany or Italy. These spectacular skeletons were supposedly the remains of martyrs—people who died because they refused to give up their religion. Their remains, referred to as relics, are considered holy. Some people believe that God uses them to perform miracles, like healing an illness, or to provide divine protection.

IT COULD TAKE NUNS OR MONKS YEARS TO COMPLETELY DECORATE THE SKELETONS.

NECROTECH

Human beings have always looked to new technology for ways they can preserve memories, continue relationships, and even communicate with the dead. Technology relating to death is known as necrotech. Today, we have access to more digital memories than ever, including photos and videos. While this provides us with wonderful options for necrotech, we should also remember that what makes our relationships with other people so precious is that they can't be recreated. They belong to you, forever.

OLD INVENTIONS

One of history's greatest inventors, Thomas Edison, had been working on an idea for a "spirit phone." He wanted to create a device that would allow him "to see if it is possible for personalities which have left this Earth to communicate with us." Edison believed that although a person's physical body died, their personality might continue to exist as another form of energy that could be communicated with through his invention.

IN THE PAST, FAMILIES WOULD OFTEN HAVE A FINAL PHOTOGRAPH TAKEN OF THEIR LOVED ONE AFTER DEATH.

TOMB-SWEEPING

During the Qingming festival, also called Tomb-Sweeping Day, people of Chinese ancestry clean their ancestors' graves, leave offerings, and perform ancestral rites. When cemeteries were closed during the COVID-19 pandemic, websites allowed people to leave virtual offerings and messages at digital graves.

HOLOGRAMS

These 3D images, created by bouncing a laser off a solid object, are no longer something that can only be seen in sci-fi movies! Today there are companies that work with living people to create hologram messages that can be played at their future funerals.

VIDEO GAMES

Game developers have created countless games that can help us explore mortality and understand death. Gamers have used games as a way to grieve, hold funerals, and create cemeteries or memorials. They have also created special characters and worlds named after a person or pet they want to remember.

GLOSSARY

AFTERLIFE
A destination that some people believe a person's soul goes to after their physical body dies.

AQUAMATION
The process of reducing a dead body to ashes and bone using alkaline water and heat.

ASHES
The substance that remains after a person's body is cremated or aquamated.

CASKET
A large box in which a person's dead body is placed before they are buried or cremated.

CATACOMB
An underground cemetery.

CEMETERY
A space where dead bodies are buried, also called a graveyard.

COFFIN
A six-sided box for holding a person's dead body before it is buried or cremated.

COLUMBARIUM
A building for storing cremated remains.

CORPSE
A dead body.

CREMATION
The process of reducing a dead body to ashes and bone by fire.

CRYPT
An underground room or chamber where dead bodies are kept.

DECEASED
A person who is dead or no longer living.

DECOMPOSITION
The process of decay that happens to all living things once they are dead.

EMBALMING
A procedure that delays decomposition.

EPITAPH
Words that are carved into a person's headstone.

FUNERAL

A gathering, sometimes involving a ceremony, where people honor a person who has died.

FUNERAL RITES

Rituals or traditions that are performed at funerals.

GRAVE GOODS

Personal items, or objects of religious or cultural importance, that are placed with a body before burial or cremation.

GRIEF

The feeling, or combination of feelings, we experience after someone dies.

HEARSE

A type of vehicle that is used for transporting dead bodies.

INTERRED

When a dead body is placed into a grave or tomb.

MAUSOLEUM

A building or structure where dead bodies or cremated remains are stored.

MEMORIAL

An event or object to honor someone who has died.

MUMMIFICATION

The process of preserving a dead body.

OSSUARY

A box, building, or other structure for holding or displaying the bones of the dead.

PALLBEARERS

The people who help carry the casket, coffin, or person's dead body at a funeral.

PSYCHOPOMP

A being who guides a person who has died to the afterlife.

REPAST

The meal that follows a funeral.

SHROUD

A cloth that's used to wrap a corpse in for burial or cremation.

INDEX

This has been a

NEON  SQUID

production

For my ancestors... and yours.

Author: Sarah Chavez
Illustrator: Annika Le Large

Editorial Assistant: Malu Rocha
US Editor: Jill Freshney
Proofreader: Georgina Coles
Indexer: Elizabeth Wise

Created for St. Martin's Press by Neon Squid
The Stables, 4 Crinan Street, London, N1 9XW

EU representative:
Macmillan Publishers Ireland Ltd,
1st Floor, The Liffey Trust Centre, 117–126
Sheriff Street Upper, Dublin 1, D01 YC43

10 9 8 7 6 5 4 3 2 1

Printed and bound in Guangdong, China
by Leo Paper Products Ltd.

ISBN: 978-1-684-49375-3

Published in March 2024.

www.neonsquidbooks.com